THE COMPLETE
FLY-TYING BOOK

Copyright © 2007 by becker&mayer!

Library of Congress Control Number: 2007937934

ISBN: 978-1-60380-010-5

Printed in China

Design: Kasey Free
Editorial: Kjersti Egerdahl
Production Coordination: Leah Finger and Jason Astrup
Project Management: Sheila Kamuda

10 9 8 7 6 5 4 3 2 1

becker&mayer! Books
11010 Northup Way
Bellevue, Washington 98004

www.beckermayer.com

THE COMPLETE
FLY-TYING BOOK

LEARN TO TIE FIVE FLIES • *by Steve Probasco*

CONTENTS

INTRODUCTION

Nearly everyone who fly-fishes will, at some point, get the urge to tie his or her own flies. There is great satisfaction in catching fish with hand-tied flies. Tying your own will also save you plenty of money—in a hurry! In addition, fly tying is just plain fun: hours on end can be spent creating at the fly desk.

In fly-fishing, you're not limited to any particular species. There are lines and fly patterns that will let you fish for just about anything that swims. In general, flies are tied to imitate the naturally occurring foods of fish. Regardless of what species you're after, flies can be tied that exactly imitate, or generally emulate, its food. From aquatic insects, terrestrial (land-born) insects, and baitfish to frogs and mice, fish eat a wide variety of available foods, and the fly-tier—with a little practice—can duplicate any of them.

By reading this book and using the basic kit materials provided, you will learn how to tie five basic flies for trout and panfish: the Woolly Bugger, Dragonfly Nymph, Carey Special, Pheasant Tail Nymph, and Peacock Soft Hackle. Moreover, with the skills you learn by tying the flies featured in this book, you will be able to tie hundreds of standard patterns, as well as create your own flies for trout, panfish, or any other fish. All of the skills you use in tying the five flies featured in this book will be used whenever you tie flies.

In addition to these basic skills, there are many advanced techniques used when tying more complicated patterns or patterns using different materials than those covered in this book. For example, some flies imitate the natural food items of fish, but some flies, called attractors, don't really imitate anything; rather, with their movement, flash, or color, they entice fish into striking. Once you master basic skills, you will undoubtedly want to learn more—and so a selection of outlines for more advanced flies appears at the end of this book.

The step-by-step instruction and photography in this book make learning to tie flies a simple, enjoyable adventure. By the time you finish this book, you will be well on the way to becoming a fly-tier. Each time you create a new fly that fools a fish, the drive to tie your own increases.

KNOW YOUR INSECTS

Aquatic entomology, the study, classification, and collection of insects, is very important to the fly fisher. Only a handful of aquatic insects concern the angler; the successful fly fisher must be cognizant of their life cycles, availability, and fish appeal.

Trout, like most other fish, are opportunistic feeders. They feed on nearly any food item in abundance, although they prefer some insects and food items over others. The major aquatic insects are mayflies, stone flies, caddis flies, dragonflies, damselflies, and midges. Terrestrial creatures to know include ants, beetles, grasshoppers, and inchworms. Also of major importance to the trout and the fly fisher are foods such as leeches, crustaceans, snails, other fish, and worms.

In general, knowledge of the basic food items of trout—their size, shape, color, and movement—is a starting point for tying flies that imitate these basic foods. It is important to keep in mind that these food items come in a variety of sizes, and that the trout will often key in on one particular size. This is especially true with aquatic insects.

Understanding the life cycle of the aquatic insects is very important to the fly-fisher. The various stages not only look different, but also move differently in the water. Most insects exist within a life cycle beginning with an egg that hatches into a juvenile, or nymph. These nymphs eventually mature, leave the water, and turn into adults. Adult insects return to the water to lay eggs and renew the cycle. Some aquatic insects, like the caddis fly, undergo complete metamorphosis:

egg to larva to pupa to adult. The successful fly fisher will understand the basic shape, color, and movement of each stage.

A good way to begin understanding aquatic insects is to go out and actually collect them.

Subaquatic forms can be collected from a stream with a piece of door screening attached to dowels: Hold it crossways in the stream while scuffing the streambed upstream with your feet. Dislodged insects will float into the screen, where they can be removed from the water and analyzed. Floating insects can also be caught with a small aquarium screen. Insects in still waters can be collected around shallow shorelines using a small net. Flying insects can be nabbed with your hat. Many fly fishers carry small jars with them so they can take their specimens home to use as examples while tying flies.

It is important not only to observe the size, shape, and color of these key insects, but also to note their movement in the water. Place the captured specimens in a calm, shallow area, and watch how they swim or crawl. Imitating this movement will be as important to successful fishing as selecting the right size and color of fly.

Once you have a general understanding of the aquatic insects and other food items available to the trout, tying flies to imitate them will be much easier. For a basic reference, here are a few characteristics of the major aquatic food items of the trout.

AQUATIC SPECIES

A. MAYFLIES

Mayflies are found in both moving and still waters. The nymph lives in the water for approximately one year. Mayfly nymphs are a major food item of the trout, and imitations are of great importance to the fly-fisher.

There are several varieties of mayflies, but the nymph of most mayflies can be imitated with very basic nymph patterns, such as the Pheasant Tail Nymph featured in this book. Most nymphs are brownish in color, although other common colors include black, yellow, and olive.

As the nymphs increase in size, they shed their skins several times. Just before emergence, the adult forms inside the nymphal shuck. The wing pads enlarge and grow dark in color. It then swims to the surface, where it hatches into the dun stage. Duns are usually drab in color.

While sitting on the water, duns hold their wings high, like tiny sailboats. One day later, the dun molts to become the sexually mature spinner. Spinners have glossy bodies and clear wings. They can be found in several colors. The spinners fall onto the water to lay eggs, and their wings fall to their sides, causing them to resemble airplanes.

B. STONE FLIES

The stone fly nymph lives in highly oxygenated moving water for one to three years. Nymphs can be large—up to a couple of inches in length. Most are dark brown to black on the back, slightly lighter on the underside.

When ready to hatch into the adult stage, the nymph crawls to shore, and the adult emerges, usually at night. The Woolly Bugger featured in this book could be mistaken for a stone fly nymph when fished in fast-moving streams.

The adults vary in color with species—there are more than 460 North American species of stone fly. Common colors also include green, yellow, orange, gray, rust, and brown. The female lands on the water to lay eggs, and this usually causes an all-out feeding frenzy.

C. CADDIS FLIES

The larva lives in the water for one year, after which it seals itself in a case on the stream's bottom and becomes a pupa. After a few weeks the pupa cuts free of the case and swims to the surface, where the adult emerges. Pupas range in color from tan to green to brown to rust. During this emergence, the caddis fly is in great peril. Soft-hackled flies like the Peacock Soft Hackle featured in this book are highly effective during the emergence. Females land on the water to lay eggs, renewing the life cycle.

D. DAMSELFLIES AND DRAGONFLIES

Nymphs live in the water for one or two years. Although similiar in appearance and color (shades of green and brown), the dragonfly nymphs are much larger than the damselflies. Mature nymphs swim (damselflies) or crawl (dragonflies) to land, and then the adult emerges. Both nymphs are most vulnerable during emergence.

The dragonfly nymph is realistically imitated with the Dragonfly Nymph featured in this book. The damselfly nymph can be emulated with both the Carey Special and the Peacock Soft Hackle when tied in small sizes.

Although female damselflies and dragonflies deposit eggs on the water, the adults are not as important to trout as the nymphs.

E. MIDGES

The larval stage lasts up to a few months. The next stage, the pupa, is free-swimming and moves up and down in the water column. The pupal stage is very important to the fly-fisher, as it is available in great numbers all year long. They are found in a variety of dull earth tones, but black is the most prevalent. Adults emerge at the surface, and females return to the water to lay their eggs on the surface.

F. LEECHES

Most leeches live near the bottom and may reproduce several times per year. Shades of brown, green, and black are most common. The Woolly Bugger is a very good leech imitation—and trout love leeches.

G. FOOD FISHES

Smaller fishes are usually found in weedbeds and shallows. Trout will eat other fishes, and some of the larger fishes in the river or lake will take minnow imitations. Scuds, or freshwater shrimp, live in shallows, down to ten feet. Wherever you find scuds, you will find a healthy population of trout, as they are a favorite food. A small, soft-hackled fly like the Peacock Soft Hackle will do a fair job of imitating these erratic swimmers.

TOOLS AND MATERIALS

The modern fly-tier has myriad tools and tying materials from which to choose. New tools and fly patterns are constantly being developed, and the fly-tier of today needs to stay aware of what's available.

In this section, I mention only a few of the common tools and materials in use. It would be impossible to name every tool and material used in fly tying—the list would be a mile long. Use this section as a general guide when selecting tools and materials, but don't be afraid to experiment and try new things on your own. Who knows, you may come up with a revolutionary new material or tool that makes some technique easier.

This kit provides the basic tools and materials; the intention is simply to introduce you to the art of fly tying, by supplying everything you need to tie five simple patterns.

TOOLS Your tying tools are very important. From the basic tools, such as those included in this kit—vise, bobbin, hackle pliers, and whip finisher—to the specialized tools needed for more advanced fly tying, your tools make certain aspects of fly tying much easier.

MATERIALS The list of body materials available to the fly-tier is endless. The most common items used are floss, chenille, wool, spun fur, and several synthetic materials, which come wound on small cards.

Dubbing materials are various furs and synthetics that are twisted to the tying thread to form a very natural-looking body material.

Many different types of feathers, hairs, tails, and synthetics are used in fly tying, creating everything from wings and tails to legs and antennas of various insects.

Using this kit, you will be able to tie five flies using these few materials: marabou (one fuzzy olive feather), saddle hackle (six dark olive feathers), pheasant rump feathers, pheasant tail feathers, peacock herl, chenille, copper wire, and black thread.

Following are close-ups of the tools and materials you will be using. You should refer back to these photos as you tie.

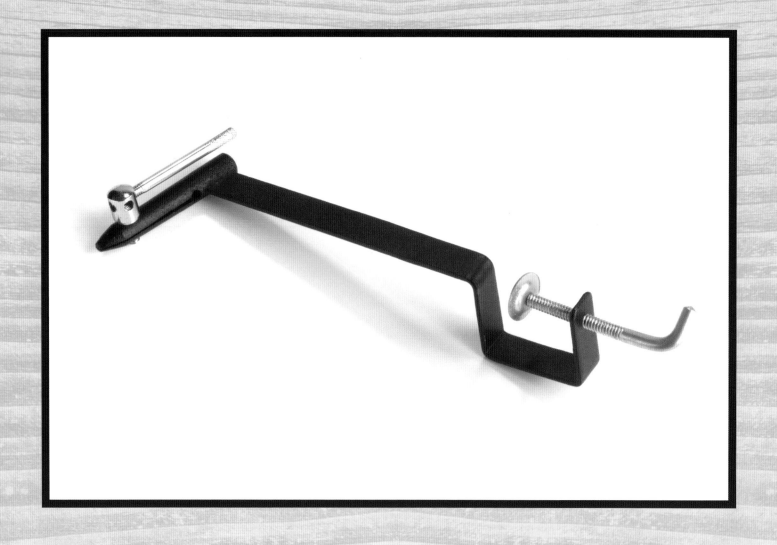

VISE | The most important tool in any fly tying kit is the vise that holds the hook during the tying process.

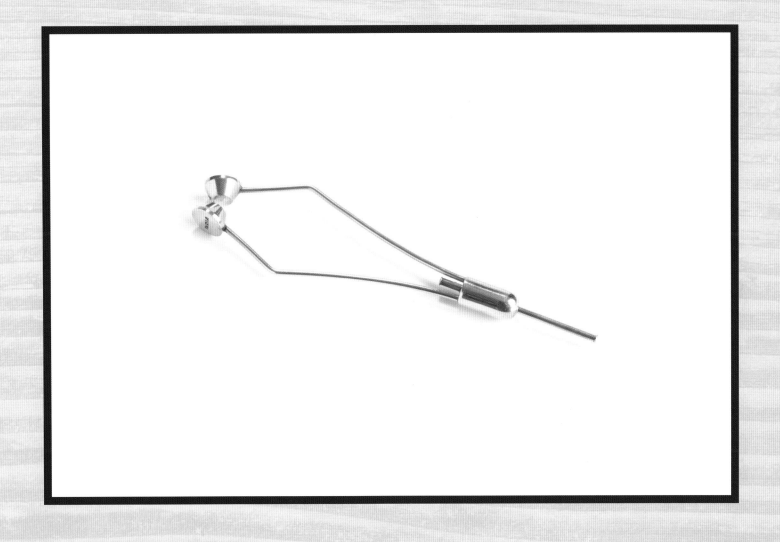

BOBBIN

The bobbin holds your tying thread and keeps it under constant tension.

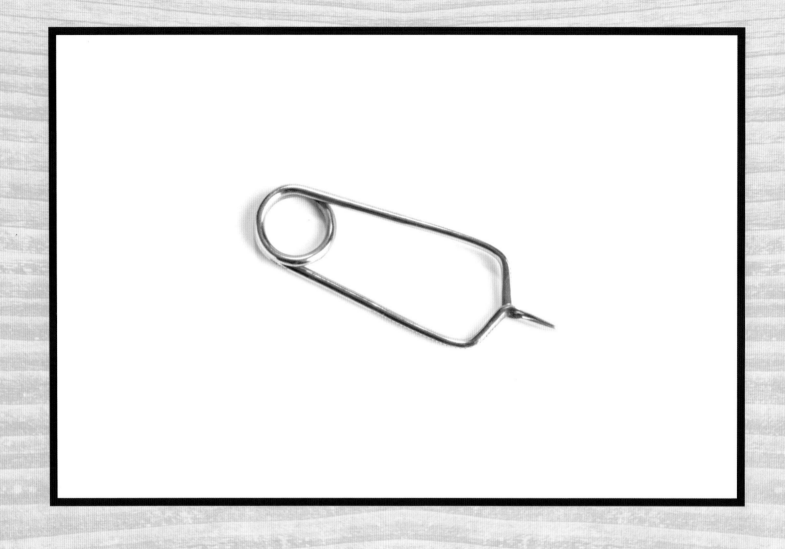

HACKLE PLIERS

Hackle pliers are used to grip the hackle (feather tip) while it is wound around the hook.

WHIP FINISHER

This tool allows you to tie a knot rapidly, securing the thread at the head of the fly.

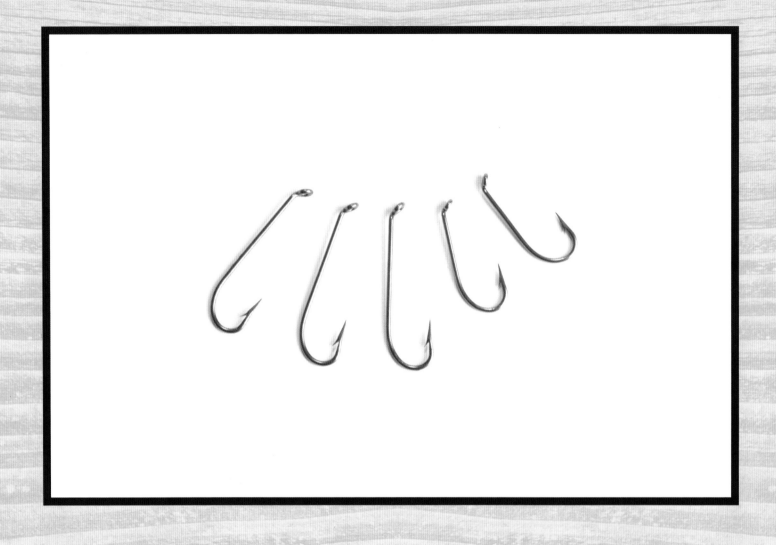

HOOKS

This kit contains two different sizes of hooks: The long hooks will be used for tying the Woolly Bugger, Dragonfly Nymph, and Carey Special, while the short hooks will be used for the Pheasant Tail Nymph and Peacock Soft Hackle.

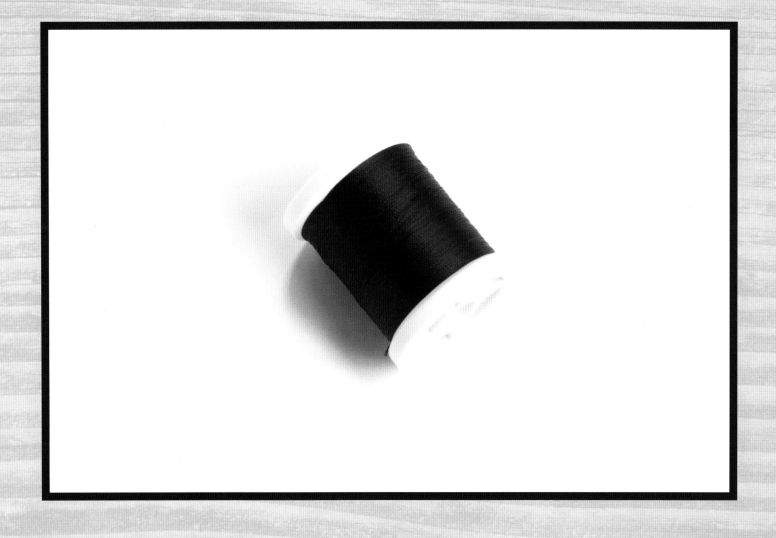

THREAD

Although fly-tying thread comes in a variety of colors and sizes, the black thread included in this kit is useful for a variety of flies.

CHENILLE | The chenille will be used to form the body of the Woolly Bugger, Dragonfly Nymph, and Carey Special.

COPPER WIRE | The copper wire is used for the ribbing on both the Pheasant Tail Nymph and Peacock Soft Hackle.

20

FOAM DISPLAY PEDESTAL

Push the hook end of each completed fly into the back of the foam display pedestal, opposite the sticker, so that each fly sits safely above its silhouette. The colors and details of your flies will stand out against the blue background.

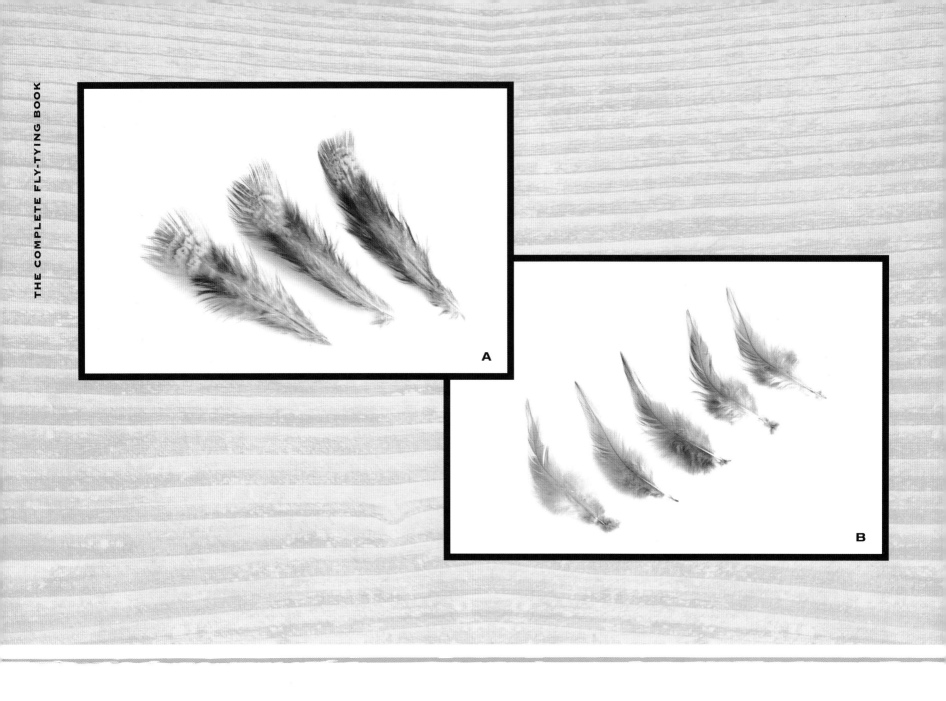

A. PHEASANT RUMP FEATHER

This rust-colored rump feather will be used as the hackle on the Carey Special.

B. SADDLE HACKLE

The olive-colored saddle hackle will be wound on the Woolly Bugger, Dragonfly Nymph, and Peacock Soft Hackle.

C

E

D

c. MARABOU

This soft, dark olive-colored turkey marabou feather will be used for the tail on the Woolly Bugger.

d. PEACOCK HERL

Peacock herl will be used to form the body of the Peacock Soft Hackle and the thorax of the Pheasant Tail Nymph.

e. PHEASANT TAIL

This pheasant tail will be used to form the tail, abdomen, thorax, and legs of the Pheasant Tail Nymph.

OTHER USEFUL TOOLS

A. HAIR STACKER

When you're tying with hair, this is an invaluable tool.
Its job is to align the hair tips before tying onto the hook.

B. CANDLE

Any type of candle will work to melt fishing line into mock
eyes, as with the large-eyed Dragonfly Nymph.

C. HEAD CEMENT

Although it's not absolutely necessary, head cement
will make the head of your finished fly much more durable.

D. MONOFILAMENT LINE

50-pound-test monofilament line is used to make the
eyes of the Dragonfly Nymph.

E. DUBBING TWISTER

This tool will help you to make thick fur bodies.

F. BODKIN

This tool is used for applying head cement and picking
out dubbing fur.

G. MATERIAL HOLDER

This spring clip attaches to the vise just behind the
jaws to hold long materials out of your way.

H. SCISSORS

Fine-point scissors are a must for all delicate work.

I. BOBBIN THREADER

Using this inexpensive tool is another way to
thread the bobbin.

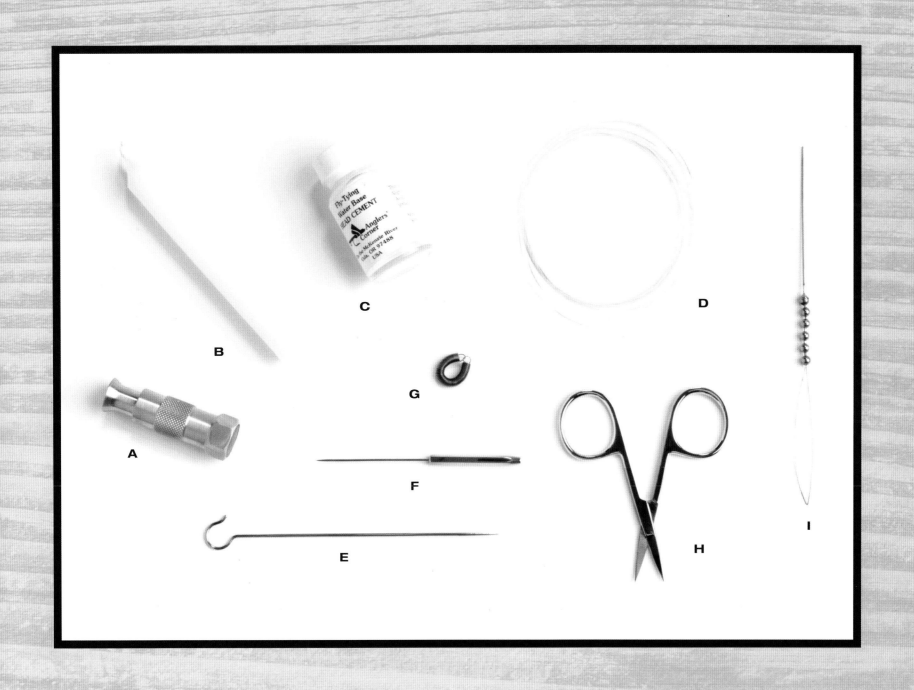

BASIC TECHNIQUES

There are a few basic techniques you should be familiar with before attempting to tie any of the flies in this book. Some involve the tying tools and their proper use. Although none of these techniques is difficult, learning them beforehand will certainly make tying the flies more enjoyable—and as simple as following a recipe. Each fly calls for different materials to be tied onto the hook in a variety of ways. Practice these techniques by using the specific materials called for in the instructions for tying any one fly, or improvise using materials you have on hand.

The number-one difficulty for beginners is making materials end properly in order to tie a small, neat head. Keep this in mind as this step draws near on each fly.

Practice the techniques shown on a bare hook until they are easy. Then it will be time to tie your first fly.

Follow the step-by-step instructions, and look closely at the photographs of each step. If your fly doesn't look like the ones pictured at each step, stop and correct it. Keep repeating that step until it looks right, and remember what you needed to do to make it right. This will be valuable information down the line. Finally, have fun and be creative.

THE VISE

A fly-tying vise simply holds the hook. It must hold a wide range of hook sizes firmly and tighten easily. Attach the vise to the edge of your work table. Turn the handle clockwise until the jaws open, and insert the hook as shown, just to the barb. Rotate the handle counterclockwise until the hook is held tight. Test it by pulling on the hook with your fingers.

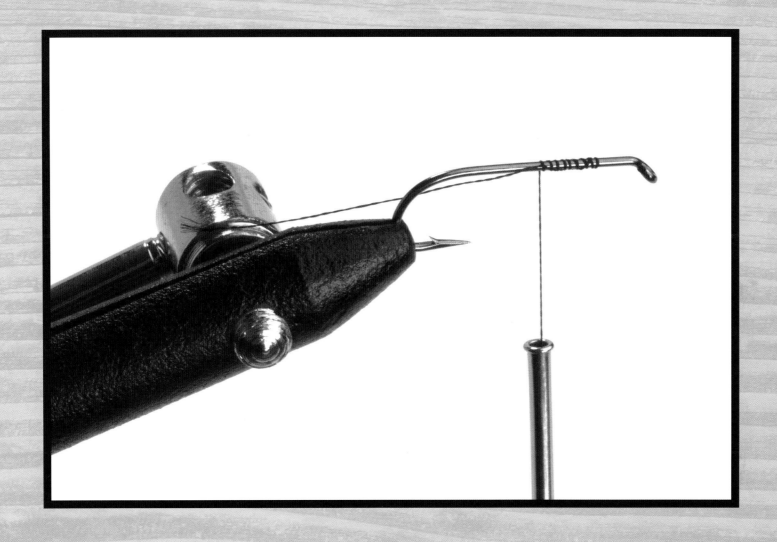

THE BOBBIN

Place the thread spool between the arms of the bobbin. If tension doesn't allow the thread to pull off evenly, remove the spool, stretch the arms of the bobbin slightly, and reinsert the spool.

Pull a strand of thread out from the spool, insert it into the tube, and push or suck it through the other side. Secure materials to the hook by revolving the bobbin around the shank, taking care to wrap the thread tightly. The hanging bobbin keeps tension on your tying thread when you are not using it to wrap on materials. Keep the thread between hook and bobbin short enough to allow the bobbin to hang fully suspended in the air.

COVERING THE HOOK SHANK

Before tying on any body materials, cover the hook shank with tying thread. Secure the thread to the hook by laying a length of thread along the hook shank and winding over it in a clockwise direction, revolving the bobbin up the shank and back down over previous wraps of the thread and finishing above the barb. This will make materials less apt to slip or spin.

THE SOFT LOOP

Use a soft loop to secure materials right on top of the hook shank so they will not roll off to the side. Hold the materials in place on top of hook shank with thumb and forefinger (you can start with a feather tip, or see project instructions for specific materials and instructions). Use the bobbin to make a loose loop around the shank and materials. Trap the loop between your thumb and forefinger. With your other hand, pull straight down on the tying thread, at the same time slowly releasing the loop to cinch materials in place. Repeat as needed.

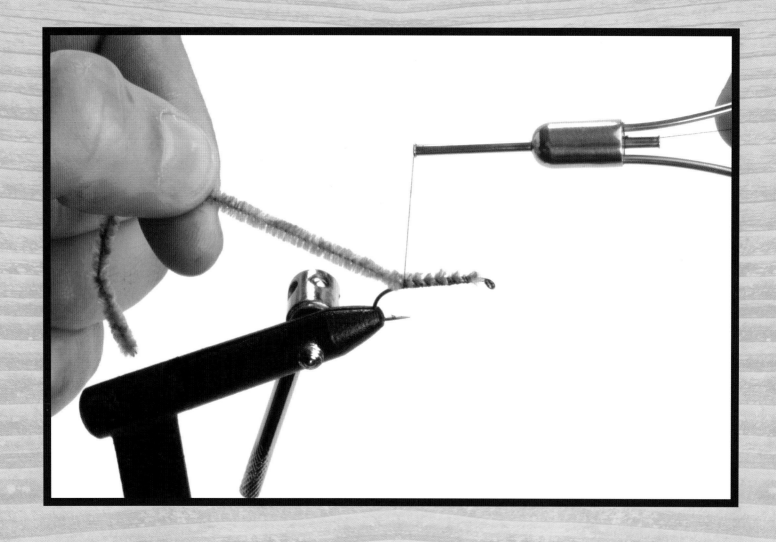

SECURING MATERIALS

When tying on body materials, secure them the full length of the hook shank by winding the thread clockwise up and down the body, according to the instructions for each specific fly.

WINDING RIB

When winding the rib (any material used to create body segments on a fly—copper wire in this kit), always wind it counterclockwise over the body material. This keeps the rib from sinking out of sight in the turns of the body material, and will better secure your body material.

THE HACKLE PLIERS

Hackle pliers clamp onto the tip of a feather segment to make it easy to wind the feather around a hook. The weight of the hackle pliers will hold tension on the feather and make it easy to wind. Squeeze the pliers, fully opening the jaws. Place the feather tip into the pliers, and release tension.

PALMERING HACKLE

Winding hackle (feathers) up the body of the fly gives the fly authentic movement. To palmer (or wind) hackle, secure one end of the feather to the hook shank with a soft loop and several wraps of thread just above the barb. Attach hackle pliers to the feather's free end and wind the hackle forward. (See specific project instructions to determine which end is tied in first.) When you are done winding, secure the hackle with several wraps of your tying thread a bit behind the eye of the hook. Be sure to leave room to wind on the fly's head.

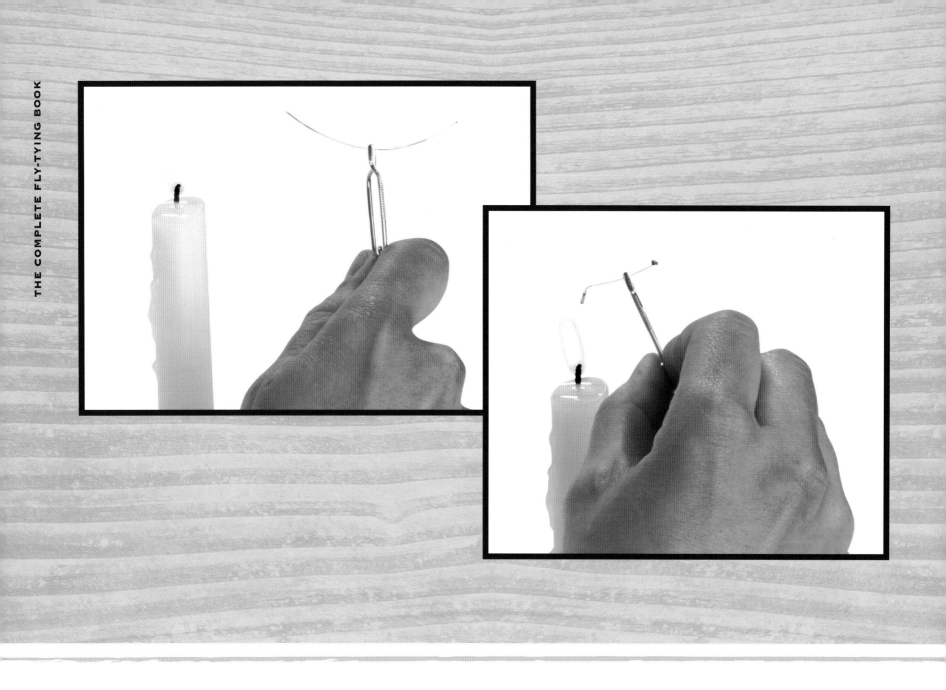

MONOFILAMENT EYES

Making eyes out of monofilament fishing line is a very effective way to emulate the eyes of large-eyed nymphs, such as the Dragonfly Nymph featured in this book. You may also buy fly eyes inexpensively at fly-fishing specialty stores. To make the eyes, hold a two-inch piece of 60-pound-test monofilament line in the center with the hackle pliers. Holding the line just over the flame of a candle and swiveling constantly in and

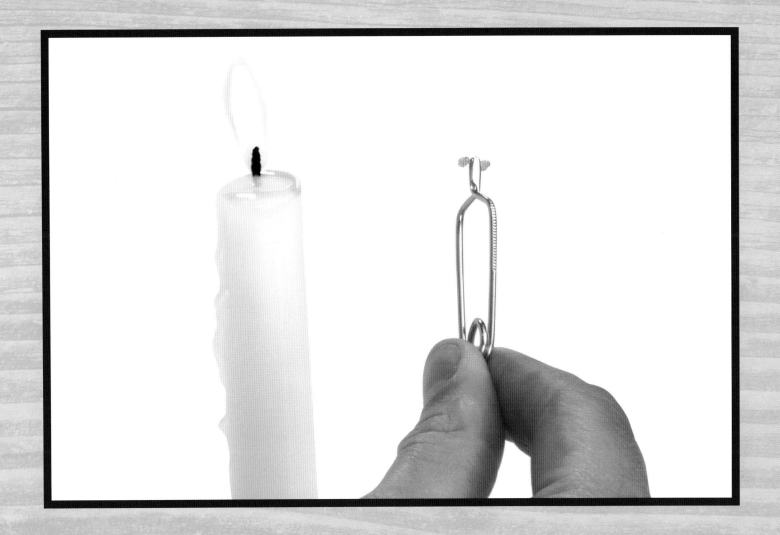

out of the heat, melt down the ends of the line to form a ball at either end. The distance between the eyes should be about the width of the pliers, but be careful not to melt them to the pliers. If the line catches fire, blow it out, let it cool, and begin again. Do not handle the eyes until they're dry, as the melted line is very hot.

THE WHIP FINISHER

NOTE: Many fly-tiers prefer to finish off their flies with a series of half hitch knots—the simplest of techniques (see page 43).

STEP 1

To tie a knot securing thread at the head of a fly, leave the hook in the vise, and attach the thread leading off the fly to the whip finisher's lower arm spring, while holding the upper arm vertical.

STEP 2 | Move the thread up and over the vertical arm, hooking it as you go.

STEP 3 | Using your left hand, lay the thread along the hook shank.

STEP 4 | Wind the lower arm around the hook shank, pivoting around the upper arm.

STEP 5 | Lift one arm up high, keeping tension on the thread with the whip finisher, and unhook the bottom arm from the thread.

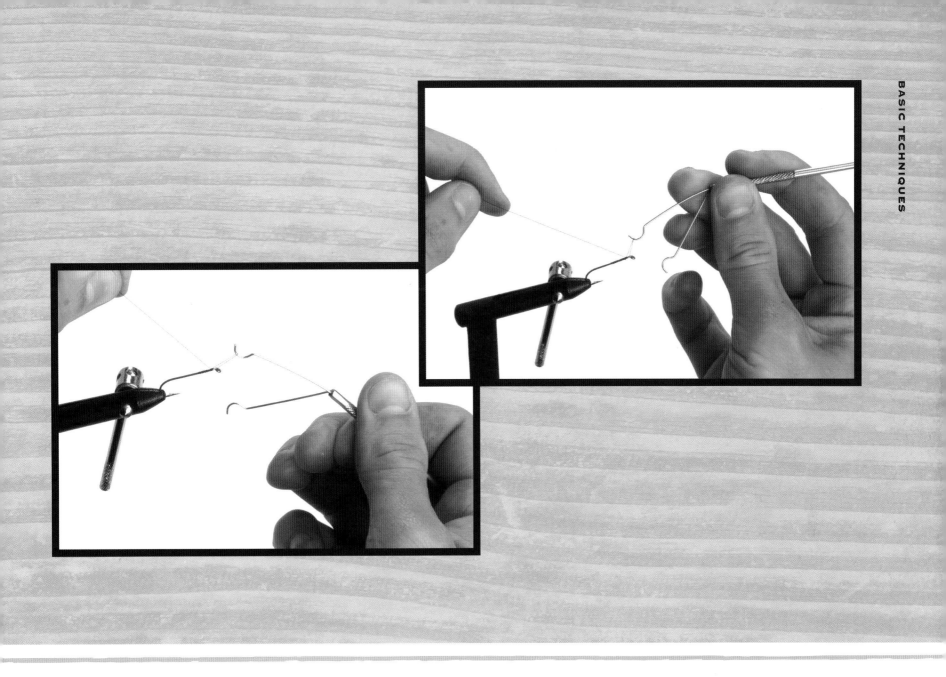

STEP 6 | Pull the thread end attached to the bobbin and hook taut with the fingers of your left hand.

STEP 7 | Pull thread tight and cinch, slipping the hook of the whip finisher out from the thread.

STEP 8 | Trim close.

THE HALF HITCH

The half hitch is a simple knot used to secure materials to your hook in place of a final whip finish. To tie one, simply make a loop around the end of your fingertip, and place that finger against the hook eye. Slip the loop off your finger, cinching it around the shank just behind the eye. Repeat several times to finish off your fly, or place the knot anywhere along the hook shank to secure materials as needed.

WOOLLY BUGGER

MATERIALS

HOOK: Mustad 33960 (long-shank hook)

THREAD: Black

BODY: Olive chenille

HACKLE: Dark olive saddle hackle

TAIL: Olive marabou

There is probably no fly more popular for a variety of gamefishes than the Woolly Bugger: It has taken a wide variety of fish species, in all corners of the world. As a trout fly, the Bugger is especially hard to beat.

Fish probably most often take the Woolly Bugger as a leech, dragonfly nymph, crayfish, or minnow, depending on the size and color in which it is tied. Fished from the top to the bottom, the Bugger produces in a big way.

Most often, the Woolly Bugger is fished on a line that will place it right near the bottom, imitating the leech. Buggers fished on the bottom should be worked very slowly. Short jerks of the line will mimic the movements of a leech inching along.

The Woolly Bugger can be tied in a variety of colors. Black, olive, and brown are three of the most popular hues, but don't overlook red, purple, yellow, or white, as these colors are also effective at times.

This is one of the easiest and most effective patterns you can use for many species of fish, including trout, panfish, and bass.

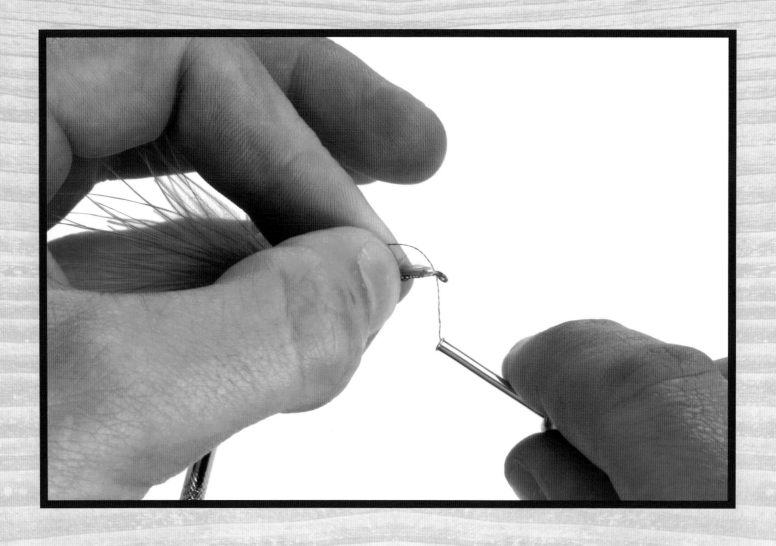

STEP 1

Cover the hook shank with thread, wrapping clockwise (see page 30).

Cut off the tip of a turkey marabou feather to a length double that of the hook shank. Lay the feather along hook shank, from a bit behind the eye to extend past the bend of the hook, as shown. Secure with a soft loop at the eye end of the hook.

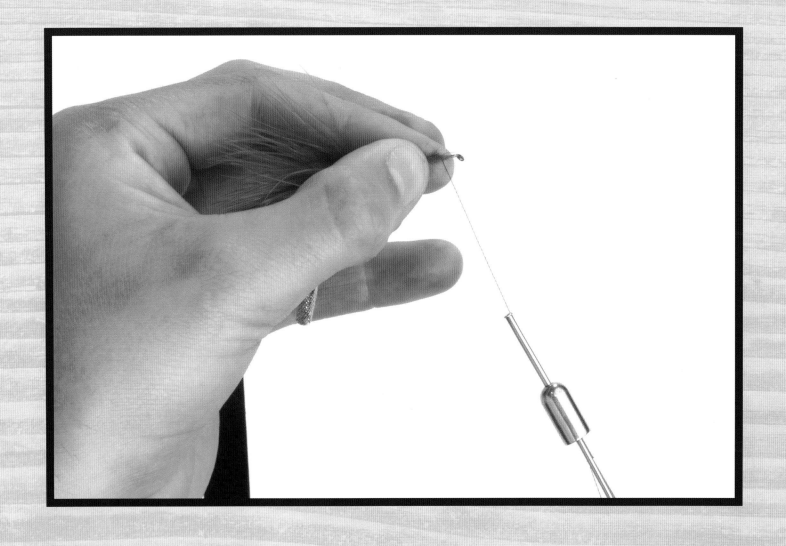

STEP 2 | Wrap the thread toward the tail, to just above the barb. Secure the feather with several wraps of the thread, and wind the thread back up to about $\frac{1}{8}$ inch behind the eye, leaving room to wrap on a head.

STEP 3

Lay a four-inch piece of olive chenille atop the hook shank and hackle, from behind the eye to just above the barb of the hook. Secure with a soft loop as in Step 1, and wrap the thread down to just above the barb and back up toward the eye of the hook. Make sure your tying thread extends to the point directly above the barb of the hook. The extra chenille will hang off to the side at the hook end.

STEP 4

Tie in an entire olive saddle hackle feather, using the soft loop method to secure the tip (not the quill end) atop the chenille, a bit behind the hook eye. As with the chenille, wrap the feather tightly with thread to just above the barb, allowing the excess to trail behind the hook. Secure the feather with several wraps of the thread, and wind the thread forward to its starting point behind the eye of the hook.

49

STEP 5 | Tightly wind the chenille forward in a clockwise direction to form the body of the fly. Stop the chenille about $1/8$ inch from the eye of the hook. Wind over the chenille with the tying thread to secure at the head.

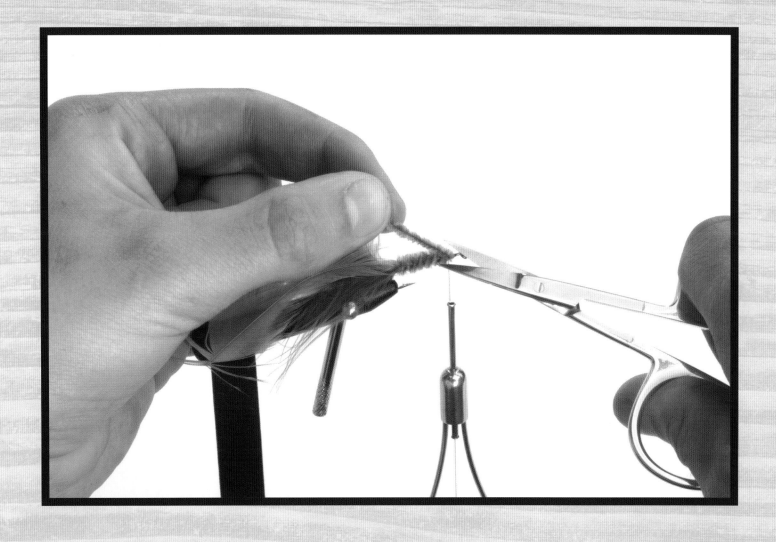

STEP 6

Trim any excess chenille; be very careful not to cut the bobbin thread.

STEP 7

Using hackle pliers or fingers, wind the olive saddle hackle forward, spacing the wraps of the feather so that it extends to the point where you ended winding the chenille, about $1/8$ inch behind the hook eye. Secure the hackle with several wraps of the tying thread at the head end.

STEP 8

Carefully trim any excess hackle at the head of the fly. Pulling the hackle fibers back and out of the way, use a series of wraps of the thread to create a $^1/_{16}$-inch head on your fly between the body materials and the eye of the hook.

STEP 9

Finish the fly with the whip finisher technique from page 38 or three to four half hitches.

STEP 10 | If necessary, trim any excess hackle from the turkey marabou feather forming the tail of the fly. You may wish to cement the head of the Woolly Bugger to increase durability (optional).

DRAGONFLY NYMPH

MATERIALS

HOOK: Mustad 33960 (long-shank hook)

THREAD: Black

BODY: Dark olive chenille

HACKLE: Dark olive

EYES: Monofilament line (40- to 60-pound-test)

The Dragonfly Nymph is one of the most productive fly patterns for fishing still waters. This big "meat and potatoes" insect is a staple in the trout's diet. A properly fished Dragonfly Nymph is seldom refused. Even during times when other insects are hatching, a big ol' Dragonfly Nymph crawled along the bottom of a lake or pond will usually put a bend in your rod.

The best place to fish this nymph is in or around weed beds. Use whatever line is necessary to get your fly down into the weeds and keep it there. Retrieve the fly slowly, working it through the vegetation. Be prepared for violent takes; trout are seldom bashful when it comes to picking up one of these morsels.

Its large eyes are the Dragonfly Nymph's most outstanding feature. The melted monofilament eyes used on this fly do a very good job of emulating nature.

STEP 1

Wrap the hook shank with thread. Starting one-third of the way down the shank, lay a four-inch piece of chenille along the hook, and secure using the soft loop technique. Wind the thread tightly around the chenille, beginning at the eye end and wrapping to just above the barb. Secure the chenille with several wraps of the thread above the barb, then wind the thread forward two-thirds of the way up the hook shank toward the eye.

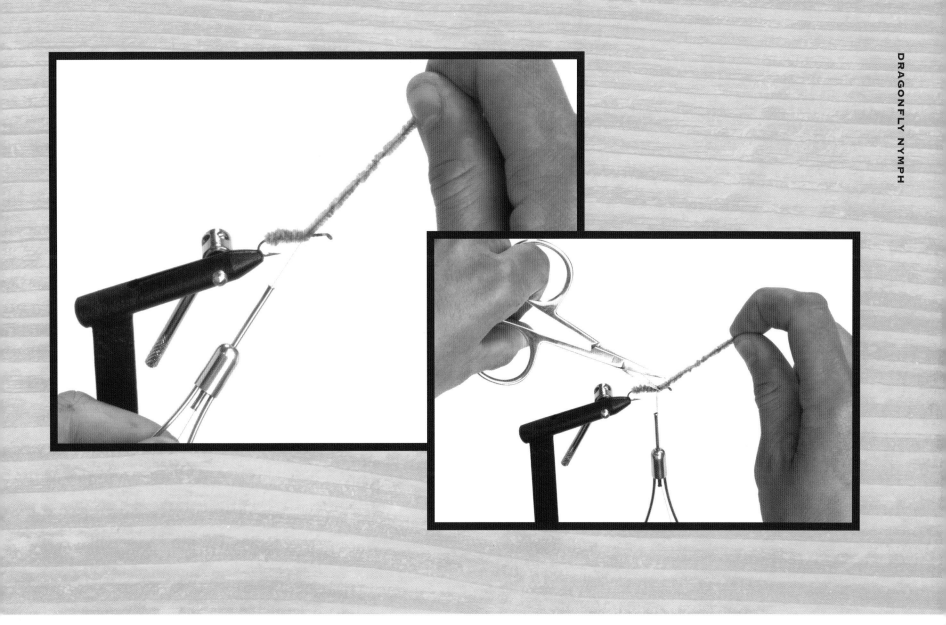

STEP 2

Wind the chenille forward tightly, two-thirds of the way up the hook shank. Secure the body materials with the tying thread, wrapping down to just above the barb and back up, all the way to the eye. Carefully trim off the excess chenille.

STEP 3

Make a set of monofilament eyes as described earlier (see page 33).

Secure the eyes to the top of the hook using a crisscross, or figure eight, motion of the thread. Once eyes are secured, wrap thread back down to where you stopped winding the chenille up the body.

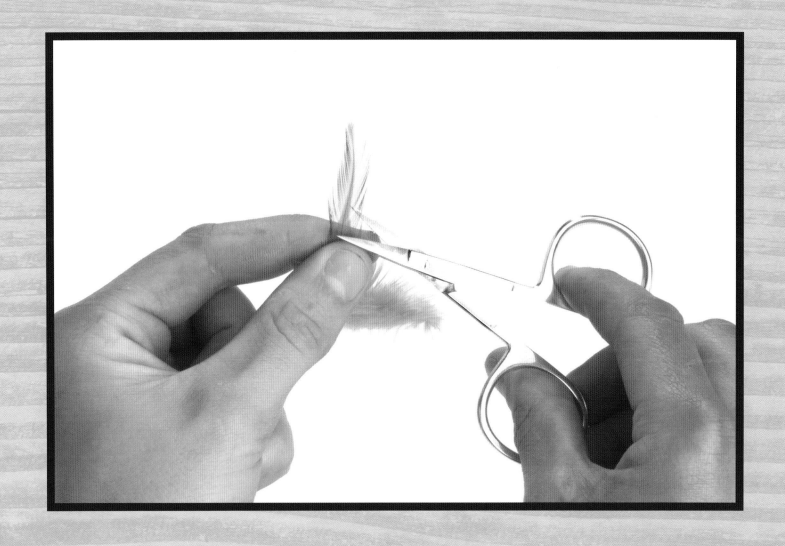

STEP 4

With scissors, clip 1 1/2 inch from the tip (not the quill end) of an olive saddle hackle, and save the tip for tying the Peacock Soft Hackle.

STEP 5 | Using a soft loop, tie the remaining section to the hook immediately in front of the chenille and just behind the eyes. Carefully clip any excess quill or fibers at the eye end.

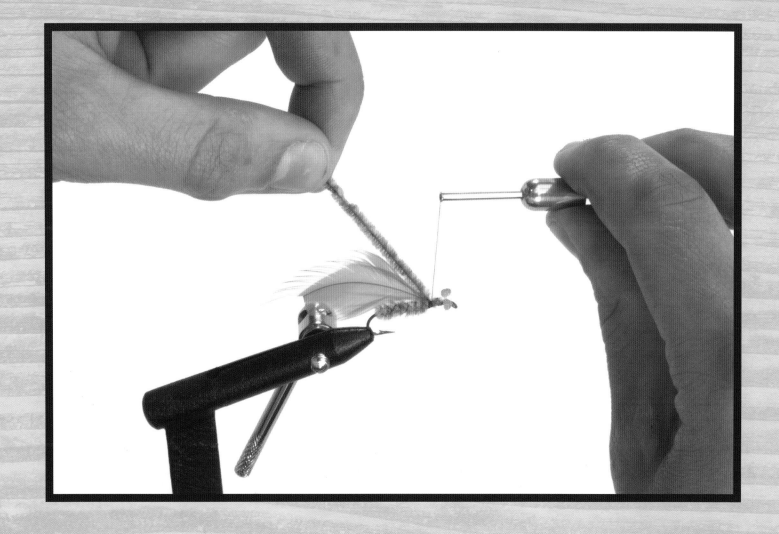

STEP 6

Tie in a two-inch piece of olive chenille in front of the hackle. Allow the excess chenille to trail forward, toward the eyes.

STEP 7

Wind the hackle three turns in place, just behind the chenille. Pull the hackle fibers and excess chenille forward with your right hand, and use your left hand to secure the hackle with the tying thread, passing the bobbin over and around. Wind the thread forward all the way to the eye of the hook.

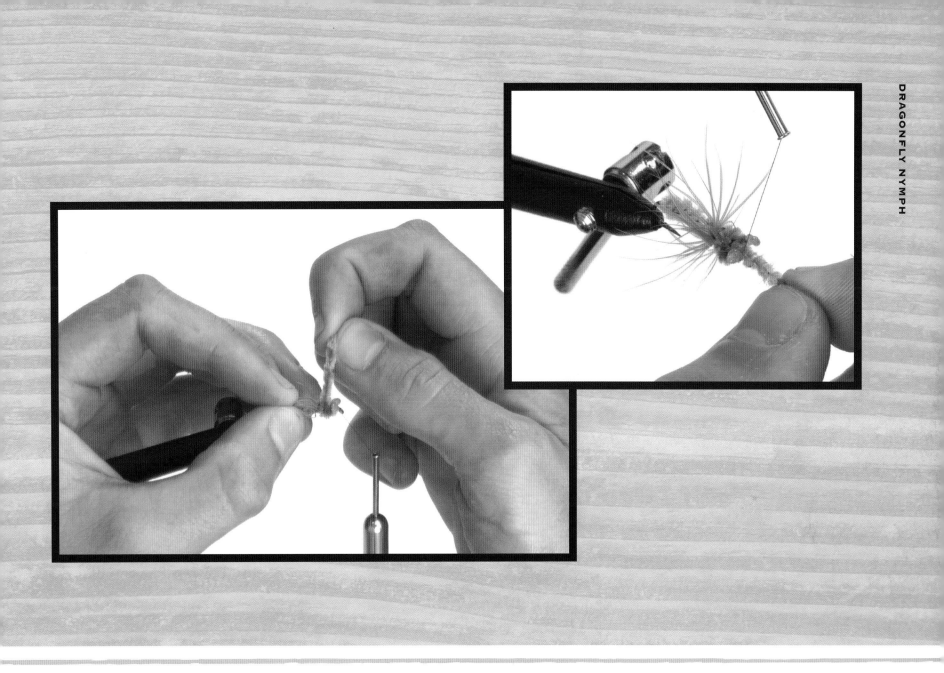

STEP 8

Pull the hackle fibers back out of the way, and wind the remaining chenille forward to the head. Pull the chenille between the monofilament eyes.

STEP 9 | Secure the chenille with the tying thread just behind the eye of the hook. Trim any excess chenille in front of eyes and behind the eye of the hook.

STEP 10

Half hitch or whip finish the head. You may wish to apply cement to the head of the Dragonfly Nymph to increase durability (optional).

CAREY SPECIAL

MATERIALS

HOOK: 33960 (long-shank hook)

THREAD: Black

TAIL: Pheasant rump fibers

BODY: Olive chenille

HACKLE: Pheasant rump feathers

The Carey Special is a very versatile fly pattern. Tied in a variety of sizes, it is suggestive of many different aquatic nymphs. It is an excellent "search pattern" and has proven itself many times over in all types of water and fishing situations.

This fly can be tied using a wide variety of body materials, but chenille is the all-time favorite. It can be tied in virtually every color under the sun. Brown, black, olive, green, yellow, and red are all popular. Hook sizes vary, of course, with the type of fish you're after and the kind of water you're fishing.

When searching new water with the Carey Special, fish it at varying depths until you locate trout. The Carey is equally at home fished with a floating line at the surface or weighted and bounced along the bottom.

The standard Carey Special is a heavily hackled fly. It is sometimes beneficial to trim the hackles with nail clippers to match the natural specimens you find in the water, and fish it along the bottom to make the fly more nymphlike in appearance.

STEP 1 | Cover the hook with tying thread.

STEP 2

Strip the fuzz from the quill of a pheasant rump feather and discard it. Strip about ¼ inch of straight fibers from each side of the quill, just above the fuzz.

STEP 3 | Lay the straight fibers along shank beginning ⅛ inch behind the eye of the hook, to extend beyond the hook and create a tail. Using the soft loop, secure the fibers just above the barb, then wrap forward to the eye of the hook and back.

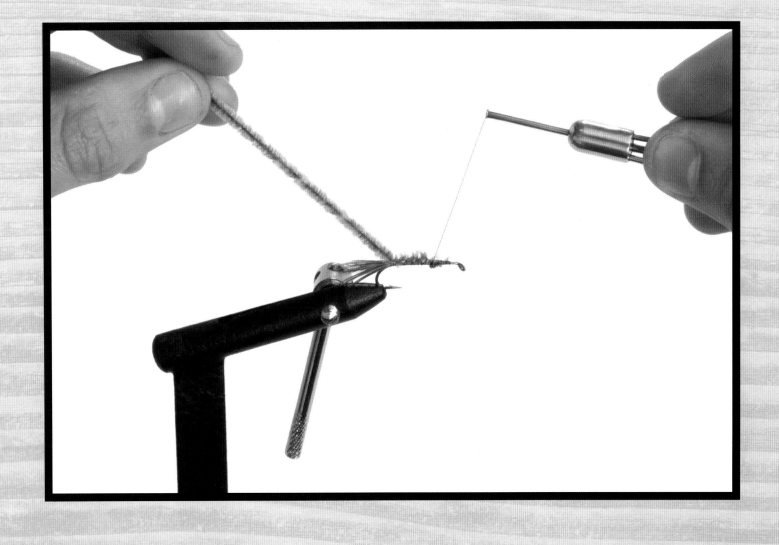

STEP 4 | Tie in a four-inch piece of chenille, securing it with a soft loop just above the barb and winding the thread forward to the eye of the hook. The excess chenille should trail back toward the tail.

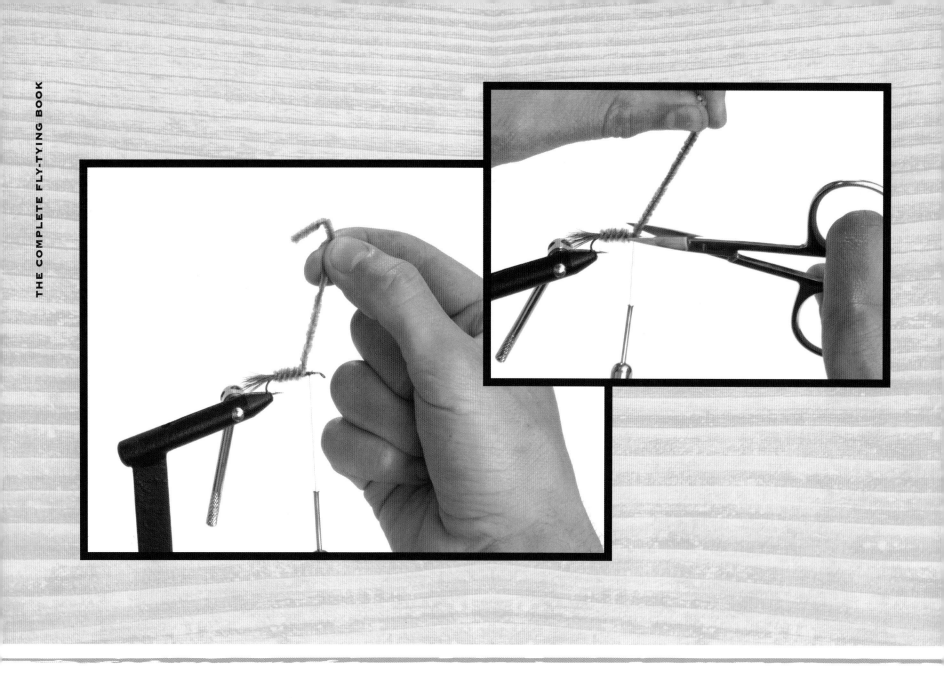

STEP 5 | Wind the chenille forward tightly, in a clockwise direction, to form the body. Secure the chenille about ⅛ inch from the eye of the hook, and secure it with several wraps of the thread. Trim the excess chenille.

STEP 6

Using a soft loop, secure the quill end of the pheasant rump feather just in front of the chenille and behind the eye of the hook.

STEP 7

Using hackle pliers or fingers, wind the hackle three or four turns in place just behind the eye of the hook, and secure it with the thread. Pull the hackle fibers forward, and hold them out of the way with your right hand. Use your left hand to bring the bobbin up and over, wrapping all materials securely.

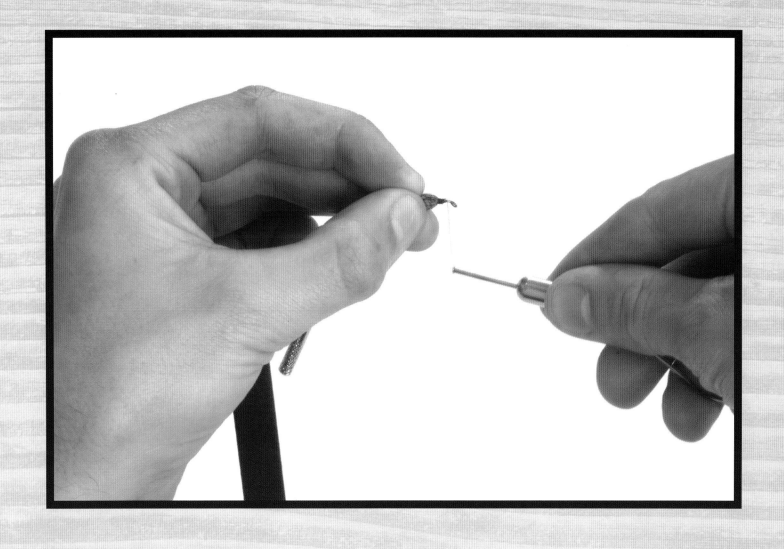

STEP 8 | Pull the hackle fibers back along the body, and wrap the thread in front of them to create the fly's head.

STEP 9 | Finish the fly with a series of half hitches, or whip finish the head. You may cement for increased durability (optional).

CLIPPED CAREY SPECIAL

For an alternative fly that's a good choice for imitating various nymphs, simply clip the front hackle of the Carey Special.

PHEASANT TAIL NYMPH

MATERIALS

HOOK: Mustad 3399-A (short-shank hook)

THREAD: Black

TAIL: Pheasant tail fibers

ABDOMEN: Pheasant tail fibers

RIB: Small copper wire

THORAX: Peacock herl

WING CASE: Pheasant tail fibers

LEGS: Pheasant tail fibers

There are a few nymph patterns in existence that just work everywhere. The Pheasant Tail Nymph is one of them. This fly is one of the best mayfly nymph imitations around—and it does a good job of imitating several other aquatic insects when tied in a variety of sizes.

The simplicity of this pattern is part of its beauty: It consists of only a couple of different materials. Because of its slim profile, it sinks rapidly. It can be fished at varying depths by using full-floating to full-sinking lines, and is effective at any depth where trout are feeding.

Keep in mind that most nymphs move slowly through the water. Fish this fly with short strips of the fly line, and pay attention to weed beds and rocky bottoms where there is an abundance of mayfly nymphs.

STEP 1 | Cover the hook with tying thread. Strip ten to twelve fibers about twice the length of the hook shank from the pheasant tail feather.

STEP 2

Lay the fibers along the hook, with the quill ends just behind the eye. Using the soft loop, secure the fibers to the hook shank above the barb. Wrap thread clockwise over the fibers to hold them onto the shank, from the barb to just behind the eye of the hook and back to the barb.

STEP 3 | Just above the barb, tie in a second small section of ten to twelve pheasant tail fibers, about twice the length of the hook shank. These should extend one length of the hook shank beyond the first tail fibers.

STEP 4

Wrap the thread forward and secure a four-inch piece of copper wire just behind the eye of the hook. Lay the wire along the hook shank, and wrap it with thread from the eye to above the barb and two-thirds of the way back up the hook shank. Excess wire should trail back at the barb.

STEP 5 | Wind the longest pheasant tail fibers two-thirds of the way up the shank, toward the hook eye.

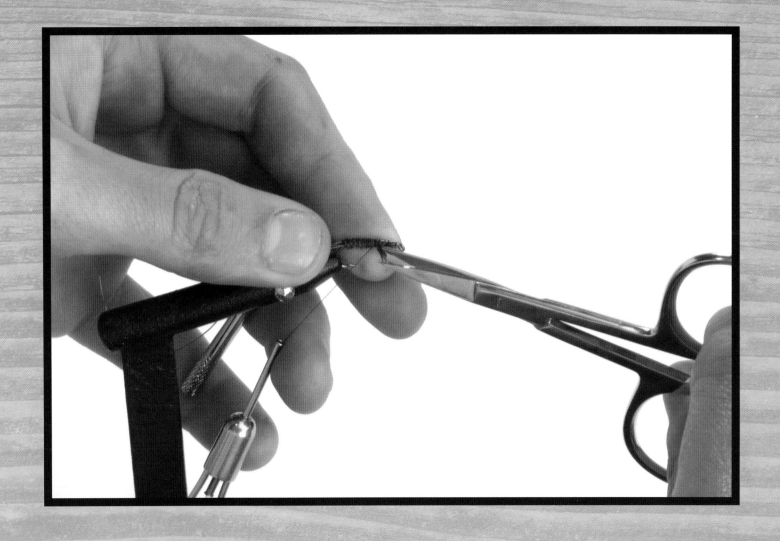

STEP 6 | Secure the pheasant tail fibers with several wraps of thread just behind the eye of the hook. Carefully trim off any excess.

STEP 7 | Wind the wire forward in a counterclockwise direction, leaving spaces between the wraps to form the rib of the fly. Secure at the same point you secured the pheasant tail: two-thirds of the way up the hook shank toward the eye. Clip the excess wire.

STEP 8

Strip off another section of ten to twelve pheasant tail fibers, and use a soft loop to tie them in where you clipped the wire: two-thirds of the way up the hook shank. These fibers should be the length of the hook from the eye to the farthest reach of the bend. They will become the fly's wing case and legs.

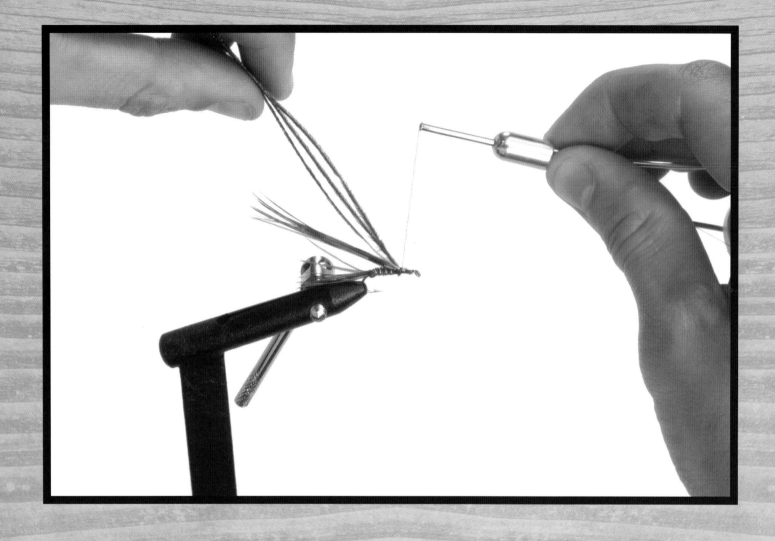

STEP 9

Tie in three strands of peacock herl just in front of the wing case, using a soft loop. Trim any excess herl sticking out of the soft loop toward the eye of the hook. Wind the thread clockwise forward to the eye. Allow the long ends of the herl to trail back off the body in front of the wings.

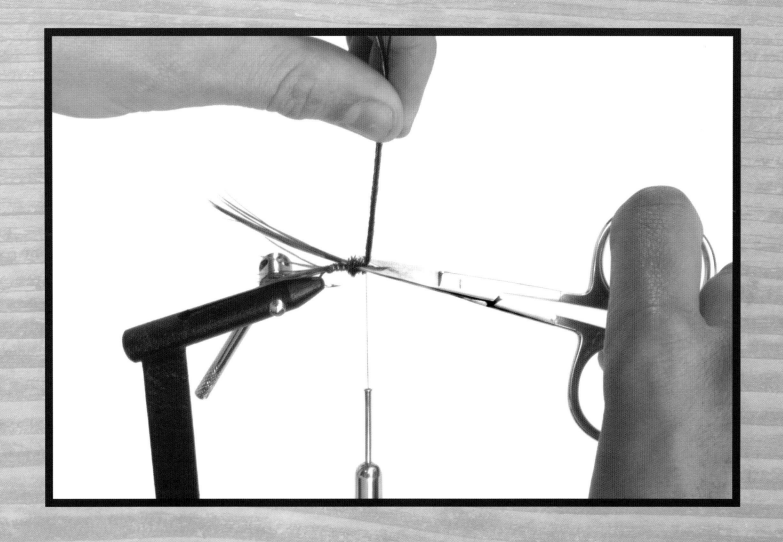

STEP 10

Tightly wind all three strands of the peacock herl forward to the head of the fly, and secure with several wraps of the thread. Clip off the excess herl.

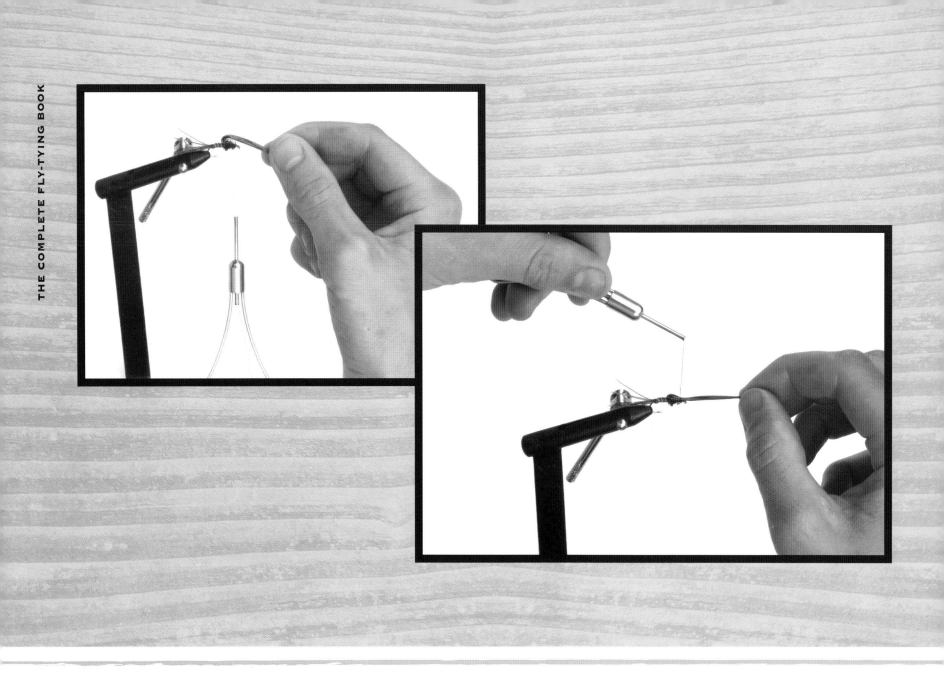

STEP 11

Pull the pheasant tail fibers nearest the eye of the hook forward, over the peacock herl. Secure the fibers atop the peacock herl with three turns of the tying thread at the point just behind the hook eye. This will form the wing case.

STEP 12 | Separate the pheasant tail fibers now extended in front of the hook eye into two equal bunches, and pull them backward along each side of the fly. Hold the two bunches in place with the fingers of your left hand.

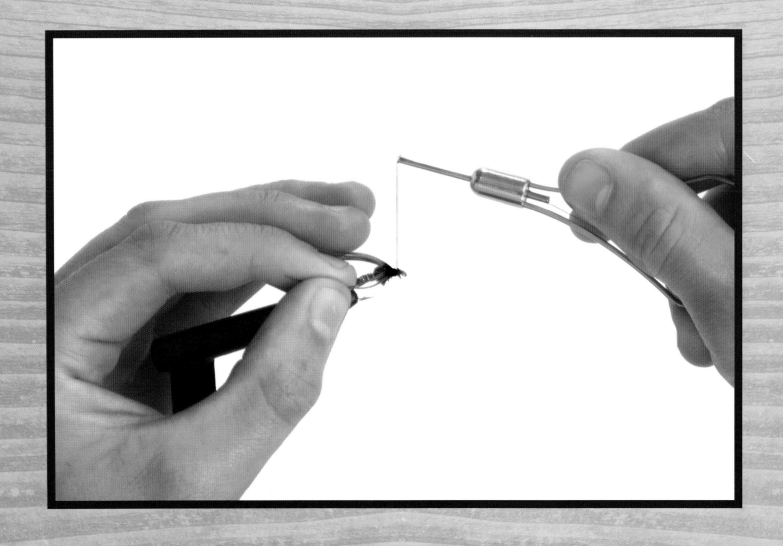

STEP 13 | Use your right hand to wrap the tying thread tightly behind the hook eye, simultaneously forming the head of the fly and securing the fibers along the sides of the body.

STEP 14

Finish the head with a series of half hitches. Cement the head if desired.

PEACOCK SOFT HACKLE

MATERIALS

HOOK: Mustad 3399-A (short-shank hook)

BODY: Peacock herl

RIB: Copper wire

HACKLE: Olive hackle tip

There are times when attempting to match a hatch exactly doesn't pan out. All of the flies that should work just don't. It is possible during these times that the fish are taking emerging insects, rather than the visible ones—when this is the case, there is no fly better than a soft hackle.

A soft-hackled fly generally resembles the pupal stage of many different insects. The long, soft hackle fibers pulsate as the fly is drawn through the water, resembling the emerging insect as it swims to the surface.

The Peacock Soft Hackle resembles the drab coloration of many aquatic insects. This is a good fly to use over weed beds, where you should slowly work the fly to the surface. It is also very effective when using the standard down-and-across approach: cast out slightly downstream and let the line swing with the current. This draws the fly to the surface as the line completes the swing. As the fly rises, it is very vulnerable.

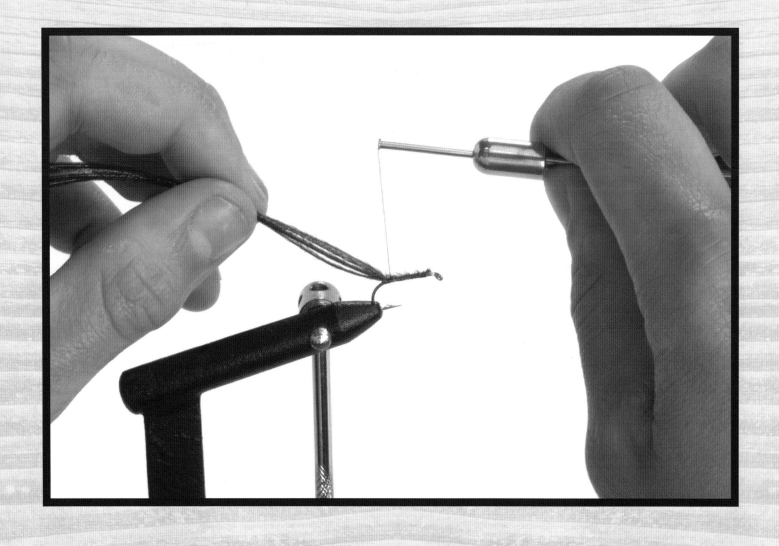

STEP 1

Cover the hook shank with tying thread. Use a soft loop to secure five strands of peacock herl on the shank directly behind the hook eye, and trim any herl that extends in front of the securing point. Lay the long strands of herl along the hook shank, and wrap them with thread to a point directly above the barb.

STEP 2

Wind the thread forward, and tie in a three-inch piece of copper wire just behind the eye of the hook. Wrap the wire with thread from the eye down to the barb, as with the herl in Step 1.

STEP 3 | Wind the peacock herl tightly around two inches of the tying thread, leading off the barb end of the shank.

STEP 4 | Wind the herl-wrapped thread forward to the eye of the hook. Free the tying thread, and secure the herl to the hook shank just behind the eye with several wraps of the thread.

STEP 5 | Trim the excess herl, being very careful not to cut the tying thread.

STEP 6 | Wind the copper wire forward counterclockwise over the peacock herl, leaving even spaces between each of the ribs. Secure the wire with thread at the head, and trim the excess wire.

STEP 7 | Using a soft loop, tie in the quill end of the hackle tip left over from tying the
Dragonfly Nymph (see page 61) just behind the hook eye.

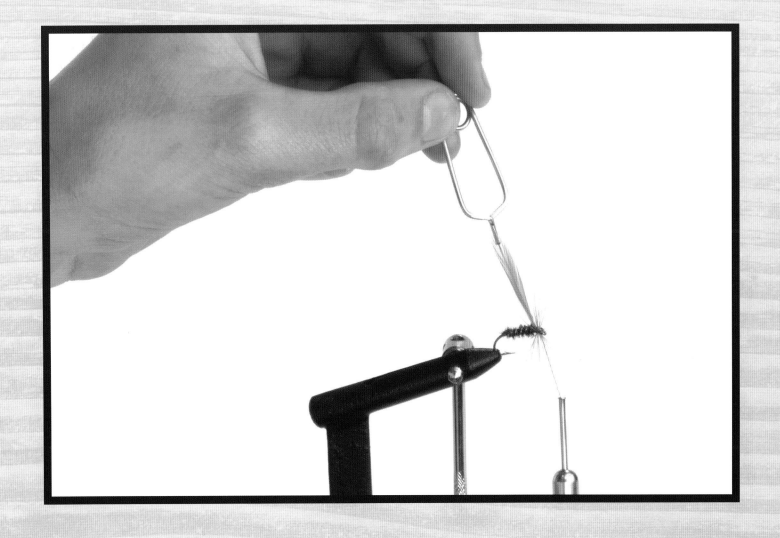

STEP 8

Attach the hackle pliers to the tip of the feather, and wind it two or three turns in one place, just behind the hook eye and in front of the body. Secure it with several wraps of the thread, and clip any excess hackle extending in front of the point where it's tied in.

STEP 9 | Pull the hackle back out of the way with one hand, and wind on a head with the thread.

STEP 10 | Use a series of half hitches or the whip finisher to tie off the head. Cement if you choose.

AFTERWORD

At this point you have learned several basic fly-tying procedures and techniques. You now know the basics for tying on various materials to create different styles of flies. The skills you have learned from tying these five flies—Woolly Bugger, Dragonfly Nymph, Carey Special, Pheasant Tail Nymph, and Peacock Soft Hackle—will enable you tie a host of other popular patterns.

All you need to do now is buy more materials, maybe a few more tools, get an advanced fly-tying book—one that demonstrates how to tie a pile of flies—and you're in business. Advanced procedures will be much easier now that you have the basics down.

The more you learn about fly tying, the more you will get into entomology, and the more creative and realistic your flies will become. In fact, tying flies to imitate the naturally occurring foods of the fish you're after will become as fun as catching the fish. Well, almost as fun.

The following is a list of productive fly patterns you can tie with your newly acquired skills:

GRAY HACKLE YELLOW

Hook: Standard length, sizes 14 to 6

Thread: Black

Body: Yellow or gold floss

Rib: Medium gold Mylar

Tail: Scarlet hackle fibers

Hackle: Grizzly, tied bushy

WOOLLY WORM

Hook: Heavy wire, 2X long, sizes 14 to 4

Thread: Black

Tail: Red hackle fibers

Body: Chenille (black, olive, red, brown, yellow)

Hackle: Grizzly saddle hackle

CADDIS LARVA

Hook: Standard length, sizes 16 to 8

Thread: Black

Body: Tan, cream, green, or brown wool

Head: Black ostrich herl

CADDIS EMERGER

Hook: Standard length, sizes 16 to 8

Thread: Black

Body: Tan, cream, green, or brown wool (match the color of the emergers found in your fishing waters)

Hackle: Partridge (one turn)

Head: Two strands of black ostrich herl

MARABOU LEECH

Hook: 2X or 3X long, sizes 10 to 2

Thread: Black

Tail: Black marabou

Body: Black marabou

Wing: Black marabou

NYERGES NYMPH

Hook: 2X long, sizes 14 to 8

Thread: Black

Body: Dark olive chenille

Hackle: Brown, palmered, and clipped off top of fly

PARTRIDGE & ORANGE SOFT HACKLE

Hook: Standard length, sizes 16 to 10

Thread: Orange

Body: Orange floss

Hackle: Brown partridge

RED HACKLE

Hook: Standard length, sizes 14 to 10

Thread: Black

Rib: Small gold tinsel or Mylar

Body: Peacock herl

Hackle: Red furnace

ZUG BUG

Hook: Standard length, sizes 18 to 6

Thread: Black

Tail: Peacock herl (three fibers trimmed short)

Body: Three or four peacock herl fibers

Rib: Small copper wire or Mylar

Wing Case: Turkey quill

Hackle: Brown hackle fibers, tied as beard

ABOUT THE AUTHOR

Steve Probasco, editor-in-chief of *Northwest Fly Fishing* magazine, is an award-winning, full-time outdoor writer and photographer living in Raymond, Washington. He specializes in fly-fishing, and his "research" takes him all over North America. Probasco's articles and photographs appear regularly in several regional, national, and international publications. He is the author of ten fly-fishing books and one video on fly tying.

CREDITS

All photos are courtesy of istockphoto.com, except for the following:

Page 11, first column, second row: © 2007 R.A. Beattie, www.fishwithra.com.

Page 68: © 2007 R.A. Beattie, www.fishwithra.com.

Page 96: © 2007 R.A. Beattie, www.fishwithra.com.